Blessed

+ BOSSED UP

SURRENDERING YOUR AMBITION SO GOD CAN HAVE HIS WAY

TATUM TEMIA

ISBN 978-0-692-17331-2

www.BlessedandBossedUp.com

Printed in the United States of America

Table of Contents

Dedication:

To every person who knows their life means something, but haven't figured out what just yet. God gave you that vision, that dream, that business for a reason. Seek Him first, and all things will be added unto you.

To the sweetest and most thoughtful man I know, my soon-to-be husband, BJ. Thank you for loving me and supporting me every step of the way. With purpose comes a lot of pressure, but your love and support give me the assurance I need to continue walking in God's best for me. I love you always and forever.

Introduction

Did You Know?

- Over 90% of businesses fail
- 92% of people don't reach their goals or potential
- *Remember the LORD your God. He is the one who gives you power to be successful, in order to fulfill the covenant, he confirmed to your ancestors with an oath. – Deuteronomy 8:18*

Recently, I went on a trip to Mexico with the 'Bossy Posse', a group of powerful women in business who I have the pleasure of being connected with. What was more beautiful than being able to vacation with a group of like-minded women who are each successful, was the fact that we all are believers as well. In a morning of worship before joining the girls on the beach, I remember praising and thanking God for answering my prayer of having connections who loved both God and business. When I was first bitten by the entrepreneur bug, I had no one who I could share my ideas, my struggles, or my excitement with. The friends I had accumulated from childhood, college, or work, were not entrepreneurs. Starting out, I was very lonely and isolated because I didn't have people to connect with that understood my mindset or yearning for more professionally. The same loneliness translated to my spiritual life. I always identified as Christian, but when I surrendered my life and ambition to God, and committed to truly live for him, I found myself alone again. As I searched for new connections, I realized that I would have to find one setting that appealed to my entrepreneurial desires and then a separate that catered to my desire to please God. There was never a place where I could get both. I found this to be odd because I thought "Isn't God the one who gave me these ideas in the first place?" We are taught to go to college, get a job, retire, and then have fun after retirement. In college, we are groomed for four years to make ourselves marketable to an employer so that we can secure a job in our field post-graduation. After four jobs within a year of graduating from undergrad, I realized that the reason I couldn't stay in a position wasn't because of the job market – it was me. Older generations would chalk this up to me being a millennial and apply negative stereotypes to why I couldn't stay at a job. But I knew I was never satisfied because God called me to be and do more than any traditional career could provide for me. So instead of looking for new positions, I began looking for purpose. I didn't grow up in church, but I did attend occasionally. Whenever I went, I saw two different extremes as it relates to wealth. On one end, I saw a great deal of poverty in churches. There was always a building fund or an offering call asking the congregation, who didn't have much themselves, to help fulfill the needs of the church. Testimonies from members always consisted of only basic needs being met, such as their bills being paid on time. The prayer requests were always rooted in struggle or a financial pain of some sort. Of course, we are to submit all of our requests to God, but I didn't see many people discuss or request much abundance. It was almost as if there was something wrong with living an abundant life. At least that's how I perceived it. I didn't know that God wanted (and promised) much more for me. As I got older and attended more progressive churches, I witnessed the complete opposite. The pastors had luxury vehicles, multiple homes, lavish church locations, and often carried the same prosperity message in their teachings. In these settings, I learned that God does want me to live an abundant life, but I still could never find any practical solutions to unlock that type of abundance in my own life. It seemed like the pastor had all of the answers that felt good in the moment, but lacked practicality. While motivating, I still left with nothing that I could implement throughout the week. Church made me feel good, but lead to frustration later in the week when my circumstances didn't align with the motivational messages of the pastor. My relationship with church was always complex in that way. I was looking for a pastor, leader, and mentor, to teach me what God needed me to do to live the life He created for me. I didn't realize that the bible says, "I (God) knew you before I (God) formed you in your mother's womb. Before you were born I set you apart and appointed you as my prophet to the nations" (*New International Version, Jeremiah 1:5*). The reason why I consistently felt let down by churches, was because I sought people, who are flawed just like me, to give me information that God wanted to give me directly. It never really occurred to me that being a Christian wasn't about the pomp and circumstance of religion; rather it's about my personal relationship with God and being obedient to the things He wants from me. The only way I could get the blueprint I was looking for on Sundays was to consult the source Himself. The same can be said about entrepreneurship. A lot of us get a business idea and go to mentors, coaches, schools, and social media, to somehow get a blueprint on what it will take to be successful. We go on a hunt to crack the code of not falling into the 90+ percent of entrepreneurs who fail. However, just as I was giving too much power to the pastors, we give too much power to experts. We get let down when we invest in a coach or an education and still aren't successful. That is because we put too much value in what someone other than God can do for us. The only one who has the blueprint is the one who is the Alpha and the Omega; the one who knows your beginning from your end; the one who knew you before He formed you in your mother's womb. Historically, we have been taught that business and faith are to be kept separate. This is why it was so difficult for me to find spaces that fed both my business and my spiritual life. I would dare to even say that is one of the most effective tricks the enemy has used to keep us on a hamster wheel of hustle, instead of on a sure path to success. As an added barrier, he uses church hurt to further separate us from seeking the wisdom of God. I've noticed that our current world has taken a dangerous shift to worshipping creations instead of The Creator, especially in entrepreneurship. The ambitious are taught the law of attraction, or giving power to the universe and separating more and more from affiliating with Christianity. The universe or any creation, is incomparable to the power of God and quite frankly, dangerous as it leaves room for the enemy to come in and wreak havoc on our minds, lives, and businesses. Goals and ambition have clouded our judgement and taken us off our God-given assignments. This is why the Lord led me to write this book. Over the last couple years, I have recognized that I was called to be an entrepreneur and fulfill a special assignment on this earth. Originally, I tried to take what God gave me and do it in my own strength. I was trying to be self-made versus being used by God. I discovered my biggest fear would be to die, get to heaven, and the life I lived, while good, didn't even scratch the surface of what God had for me. I realized that God can do exceedingly and abundantly greater than anything I can even think of, so why didn't that apply to my entrepreneurship journey as well? When I surrendered my ambition to Him, I realized how important, and lucrative it is to make God your CEO. At the end of my Mexico trip with the Bossy Posse, one of the ladies asked me how to surrender her business. She is a believer and understands the importance of God being in charge, but didn't know **how** to put Him there. She didn't know what the difference was for her to be the CEO versus God. That's the position a lot of you are in and that's exactly what I will teach you throughout this book. My prayer is that every strategy, system, and formula I provide, you implement in your life. I pray that over the next eight chapters, the Lord speaks to you in a way that He hasn't before. I pray this isn't just another book you either don't complete or put on your bookshelf, but rather an experience that changes your life over the course of each page. I pray that you get new revelations about your life, your business, and start to immediately see the fruit that is promised to you as a result of surrendering to God.

Let's get started…

Chapter 1: Becoming Blessed and Bossed Up

CHAPTER 1:

Becoming Blessed and Bossed Up

_____

When I was a kid, if people asked what I wanted to be when I grew up, 'podcaster' would have never been my answer. Even though there are hundreds of thousands of podcasts, the podcast industry is still a relatively new medium. Podcasting dates back to the 1980's under the term 'audio blogging'. It wasn't until about 2004 that the medium began to take hold with the term being coined by Adam Curry and Dave Winer.

When I first got into the podcasting world, I had no idea it would change my life the way that it has. Podcasting has given me a voice and a platform to influence people in countries that I can't even find on a map. I first began in January of 2017 under the show name, Black Girl Boss. I was new to entrepreneurship and got tired of listening to the same interviews of those who have achieved high levels of success and could no longer relate to where I was in the trenches. I wanted to create a show based on the honest and transparent journey of pursuing your goals. No fluff, no fronting as if we had it all together - just raw and real discussions about the highs and lows of life and business. This was a way for myself, and my cohost at the time, to create a bond with others who were just like us: young, black, and committed to creating a life we don't need a vacation from.

In addition to growing my new show, I also began to grow closer in my relationship with God. I started a prayer journal as a way to document my spiritual journey and get the things I was feeling out of my head and onto paper. I wanted an outlet for my thoughts and feelings while being able to go back over time, track my progress, and revisit how I was feeling at certain points. In my reflections, I was able to see that if God brought me out of the troubles I was writing about then, he could do it again.

Many times when you are knee-deep in life with so many things going on, and caught up in the hustle and bustle, you overlook what God is doing in your life. As an over achiever, I often get caught up in crossing the next thing off of my to-do list instead of taking moments to smell the roses. Starting a prayer journal allowed me to slow down, reflect, and document my wins and answered prayers. As my journals would come to an end, I created a ritual of looking back through my entries to reflect.

One particular entry that stood out the most from my first journal was dated October 11, 2016. It said:

Three things I am believing in God for:

1. A husband
2. Full-time Entrepreneurship
3. Financial Freedom

To give context of the time when I wrote this, my now fiancé and I were dating, but not discussing marriage yet. I was working in the youth program I founded, *The Queen Academy*, and had hired a business coach to assist me in becoming a full time entrepreneur. At this time, being self-employed was not realistic for me yet. I was working a decent job, but I was still living paycheck to paycheck to fund my life, as well as, my business. I even worked a side job cleaning buildings to make extra money to put into my business. I wrote this list out in faith because while it didn't seem as if these three things I asked God for were possible, I knew that I walked by faith and not by sight. This was my introduction to allowing my faith to guide me, instead of my current circumstances. The year following that entry, was my introduction to putting the necessary actions behind my prayers.

Prayer Request #1: A husband

When I submitted my dating life to God, it was because I was fed up with the way I had done things up until that point. I had met and dated nice guys, but none of them were "the one". When I wrote this in my journal, I gave up trying to find my husband myself, and asked God to just send him to me. This is the ongoing theme I have with my prayer journals: once it is written, it is submitted to God. I no longer stress myself out about the outcome. A few months after I wrote this, I met my future husband, BJ. It was an ordinary day at work and there was a handsome, yet unfamiliar face in the office. I was getting my morning coffee and he came into the kitchen to introduce himself. When I shook his hand and saw his smile, I was immediately smitten. I didn't know right away that he was my husband, but in that short encounter, I felt a peace that I had never felt before with anyone. Over the next few weeks we would get to know each other casually in the office through lunches or events. Eventually, we exchanged numbers and continued getting to know each other outside of the office. A couple of months after that, he asked me to be his girlfriend. Even though I was very fond of him, I was still hesitant to accept. We had already established that we did not want to continue the empty dating games, but instead wanted a life partner. So by him asking me to be his girlfriend, it meant that he saw me as a potential wife. I decided to ask him why he wanted to make things official and his answer gave me the confirmation that he was my husband. He picked up his bible and turned to Proverbs 31. He told me that when he thinks about what he looks for in a wife, he uses the Proverbs 31 woman as a reference. He said that he saw the same qualities in me, that were described of the virtuous woman. This answer solidified things for me. Not because it was sweet, but because he used God's word as the measuring stick for how he makes decisions in his life. I knew then that I could trust him because he would always lead me back to God. Now we are set to wed January 19, 2019.

Prayer Request #2: Full time entrepreneurship

I knew that I didn't have all of the tools I needed to become and remain a full-time entrepreneur. I decided to seek out the help of a business coach that I felt was qualified to work with me on completing this goal. Not only did I hire someone, but I did everything in my power to learn as much as I could about what it took to become and remain self-employed. With her help, I looked at the inner workings of my business and found ways to create new revenue streams and maximize profits. I also realized that *The Queen Academy* was not going to be the vehicle that took me to my goal.

One of my favorite pastors to listen to is Bishop TD Jakes. Not only is a great orator and powerful leader, but he is a successful businessman as well. In his book *Soar,* Jakes discusses how your business is never the dream. Rather, it is the vehicle that takes you to the dream. My dream was to have the freedom of my time through being self-employed, and my youth program was the vehicle I thought would take me there. He goes on to say that your current vehicle (business) may not be what takes you to the dream, but instead, it will lead you to the one that will. What TD Jakes meant was that your current idea may not be the one that creates the life you dream of, but it will lead you to the idea that does. Both are extremely important because they are a part of your overall journey. Each plays a key role in leading you to your desired destination. I had already felt like I needed to switch vehicles, but I didn't because I thought it meant I failed. I didn't realize that it wasn't failure, but rather a pivot that would ultimate lead me to God's best for me. It's never failure unless you quit the journey completely. Once I accepted that switching vehicles wasn't failure, it gave me the freedom to move on from *The Queen Academy* as being 'it', and open my mind to what God else God has for me. I eventually decided to use my marketing skills and experience to help other, new entrepreneurs build marketable brands and make more money in their businesses through digital marketing. I was able to take what I learned through my coach to create revenue streams in this business that met the criteria of what I would need to reach my dream of being self-employed. I walked away from corporate America on May 3, 2017 and by the grace of God have not looked back. Later, I will explain how through making God my CEO, I had to change vehicles once again.

Prayer Request #3: Financial Freedom

In that season, I was also intentional about seeking God on behalf of my finances. I knew living paycheck to paycheck was not God's best for me. During that time, I was introduced to the concept of tithing and by not being a tither, I left a door open for the enemy to attack my finances. Tithing was a concept that I was on the fence about initially. I wasn't sold that I needed to or should give 10% of my income to a church. It wasn't until I was given a prophetic word that I needed to tithe, that I made it a part of my lifestyle. I figured I was spending much more than 10% to things that were not of God, so why wouldn't I give God His 10% so He could bless me with wisdom in the area of my finances? It isn't about what the church does with it, it's only about my obedience. I became a tither that year and continue to give God 10% of everything I make in my business.

—

Being able to go back and cross off these prayer requests that seemed so foreign when I wrote them built up my faith and trust in God. It showed me that seeking Him wasn't just for my personal life, but my entrepreneurial journey would be blessed as well. By God answering my three requests and blessing me in countless other ways I didn't even ask for, it showed me that I can be blessed AND bossed up, at the same time.

Are business and faith separate?

I was always taught that when it comes to business or any professional setting, you stay away from discussing religion and politics. I even fell in line with that while in the corporate world; but I struggled with it when it came to entrepreneurship. Initially, my relationship with God was my own; it was something I was growing privately, and occasionally discussing on platforms like my podcast. It wasn't until my relationship with God began to blossom that I realized the two are one in the same. God didn't give me this vision for me to do it without Him. Sometimes we get so full of ourselves and our ideas that we disregard who gave us the idea in the first place. If God is the one who gave your that business, why would God not be a part of it?

When you are a believer and an entrepreneur, you operate differently. You strategize in prayer before you strategize in meetings. You fast and pray before making major decisions. You turn down opportunities that anyone else might take if God tells you, 'No'. The bible says, "Seek the Kingdom of God above all else, and live righteously, and he will give you everything you need" (*New Living Translation, Matthew 6:33*). The bible also says, "I will go before you, and level the mountains. I will smash down gates of bronze and cut through bars of iron" (*New Living Translation, Isaiah 45:2*). So according to the scripture, we have the benefit of the Most High working on our behalf. This offers a sense of peace and relief in the process, even when the world and social media leads us to believe success is achieved overnight.

I didn't realize how involved God needed to be until He began to speak to me regarding my podcast. About six months into doing the show, God began to show me little things that needed to happen. First, He revealed that I would be doing my show solo. Once again, I was terrified. One of the reasons I sought a cohost for my show in the first place was because I didn't think people wanted to listen to just me. I am a naturally laid-back person who loves to have meaningful conversations sharing knowledge and wisdom that have helped me grow. I felt that my generation, with its love for superficial things and worldly validation wouldn't take to me. I was afraid that what I had to say, without someone else's opinion on the show, wasn't worth anything. I was caught up in the "what ifs". What if our podcast numbers decline or it no longer grows at all as a result? What if this hurts my brand more than it helps it? What if no one takes my expertise seriously because now I am talking about God?

I had so many discouraging thoughts and fears that made me question if I was hearing from God. I asked God to give me confirmation if this was indeed the step He wanted me to take. I got confirmation from a variety of different sources that it was time to move on from a joint podcast to a solo one. I procrastinated on it for months, as confirmation didn't eliminate my fear and insecurities. I read somewhere once that procrastination is just slow disobedience, and I knew I had to obey God because He only has my best interest at heart. I prayed and fasted asking God to allow this decision to end well, as I valued the friendship that was built between my cohost and I. I didn't want us going our separate ways with the show to cause me to lose a great friend.

When I eventually had the conversation with her, I was so relieved at how well it went. I learned that being obedient doesn't have to be stressful and peace is a sign that we are doing the right thing. We make obedience stressful by agonizing over what God wants us to do, instead of cheerfully obliging. After breaking off the partnership, I began to ask God to show me what was next with the show. He told me the show needed rebranding, including a new name and changes to the content. God wanted to be included in the show. Not just as someone I mentioned here and there, but as a consistent theme. I prayed, fasted, had other people close to me pray, and after months of waiting to hear from God, he revealed to me the new name. The show was to be changed from Black Girl Boss to Blessed + Bossed Up.

As I consulted with God about why this needed to happen, He told me His people need to understand that not by might, not by power, but by His spirit will they be successful. He told me there are people who continue to hit glass ceilings in their life and businesses, not understanding what's wrong, when He is the missing piece. He needs to be the CEO.

God wanted to use me and my platform to reintroduce Himself to some and introduce Himself to others so they can seek Him in all things, including their business. He wants to show we can live a life of peace, fulfillment, abundance, and overflow with Him. This made me reflect on my own journey. My first business was my youth organization, then I started my consulting business. I thought I was going to just give back to the next generation, while helping entrepreneurs and small businesses build profitable brands. I had no idea there was a bigger calling on my life. I probably would have never known had I not committed to making God the CEO of my business. I would have never changed my podcast and definitely would not be writing this book. But God! He thought so much of the listeners of the show and you reading this right now, that He used your ambition to insert Himself back into your life.

I was thinking too small before I got to know God. This is why business and faith are not separate. You will always be limited if you try to put God in a box. He is the God of your life AND your business. But before you can begin to implement these things in your own journey, you must first learn how to hear from him.

How to hear from God

Job 33:14-17 New Living Translation (*NLT*)

14 For God speaks again and again,
though people do not recognize it.

As I grew spiritually, I was able to truly learn how God speaks to me. This is a subject I believe many Christian leaders don't spend enough time teaching to their flock. Discerning the voice of God versus our own thoughts or tricks of the enemy is a vital part of growing a relationship with Him. One of my favorite books to reference for this is *How to Hear from God* by Joyce Meyer. In it, she explains how God speaks to people in different ways. God may speak to someone through a still voice, nature, dreams, prophetic words, the bible, or a combination of all. What is important for us to learn is how He speaks to US. I have friends who hear from God via dreams only, but that isn't my truth. God speaks to me through His word and a still voice. If I would have tried to apply someone else's relationship with God to my own, I would spend hours searching for meaning in my empty dreams. Learning how to discern His voice can cause a bit of frustration in anyone who is eager to follow God. Early in my walk with Him, I would be hesitant to act on the things I heard. Reason being, I wasn't sure if I was hearing from God or if it was just my own thoughts. This uncertainty caused a lot of stress for me until I got Joyce Meyer's book. In my opinion, as Christians, we often get frustrated with God and just walk away instead of finding solutions to our problems. Not hearing from God doesn't mean he isn't speaking to you, it just means you have to figure out when to know it's him. It isn't a secret code to crack, rather you must be intentional about getting to know him, so you will be able to discern his voice. How to hear from God is the number one question I get from those who have heard me speak or listen to my podcast. So I used my knowledge and wisdom to create a quick system for you to determine how to discern God's voice:

Step 1: Ask for confirmation

If you aren't sure if you heard from God, ask Him to confirm it for you. That way, when He does, you can act with confidence that you are moving in alignment with the will of God. If He doesn't confirm it, you can be sure that it wasn't His plan. Confirmation can come in a variety of different ways. It may be a scripture, something someone said to you, a sermon that speaks directly to your situation, etc. God is so understanding that He knows you are struggling hearing His voice, so He will ensure that you are able to receive messages and know in your spirit that they are from Him. In the beginning of my journey, God would use one of my close friends to confirm things for me or to speak things to me that God wanted me to receive. Since I was still new to learning His voice, He used someone I trusted to confirm. He will do the same for you.

Every week before recording my podcast, I pray and ask God to use me. I knew the reason He led me to discuss faith in entrepreneurship was because there are people He needs to reach who haven't been able to hear from

Him. It is an honor to be that vessel through both my podcast and this book. God will get to you however He needs to - it is just important that you listen.

Step 2: Use the bible to fact check

An easy way to tell if something is of God or not is to use the bible as a measuring stick. If what you are hearing contradicts the word of God, it is not of God. If it aligns with what the bible says, you can be confident that you are hearing from God

Just as you know your earthly father enough to understand when something is or isn't of his character, it is the same for your spiritual father. We have to understand God's character, who He is, and how He operates, so we can be confident in knowing we are hearing from him. The most efficient way is by spending time consistently with him. Imagine a mother was in a crowded place with her child. There are lots of other children around, but when her child says, "Mom!" she knows it's hers speaking to her. Hearing from God is the same way. When you get connected with Him, just as you are with your earthly parents, you will be able to hear when He speaks to you, even through the noise.

One of the first times I was certain I heard from God was when it was time to take a leap of faith to leave my full-time job. Being self-employed was dream and I was already believing in God for it, but when I heard from Him concerning that, it frightened me. I was afraid because I wasn't ready. I had gone through my coaching program confident that my leap of faith was going to happen soon, but not at that moment.

My plan was to leave my job in July because that's when my lease would be up and I would be able to find somewhere more affordable to live to cut down my living expenses. I planned on launching my marketing consulting business a few months prior to establish more revenue streams in preparation for the leap. So when God spoke to me, I was terrified because the risk of leaving at that time was much higher than I anticipated. I will never forget when I heard from Him. I was speaking at an entrepreneur event and decided to stay after to take advantage of some of the sessions. One of the other speakers said, "What are you waiting for? What do you have to lose?" I don't remember the context exactly, but I remember those words pierced my spirit in a way I had never experienced.

I was sitting in my seat trying to wrap my head around why those simple phrases seemed to hit me so deep. I heard a small voice say, "It's time." I knew exactly what that meant; God was telling me it was time to resign from my full-time job. A part of me was sure that this was God. Yet, another part of me was so afraid. I wanted to be wrong so I could move forward with my plan – the one I was a lot more comfortable with. I used the bible as my measuring stick to fact check if I was hearing from God before actually putting in my notice. I realized that if I were to leave my job at that moment, it would be a true leap of faith. If I were to leave my job when I planned, it would be me doing it in my own strength. I would be relying on myself, not my God. I knew I had to be obedient to what I heard.

The next Monday, I sent in my resignation letter and I walked away from Corporate America. I had no idea that God would take me on an emotional journey of testing me, stretching me, and showing me exactly what it meant to be Blessed + Bossed Up.

God Qualifies the Called

I always imagined my life meaning something, but not necessarily on a grandiose scale. In my perfect world, I would be wealthy and inconspicuous. I am in no way famous now, but God has shown me aspects of my life that involve a bit of notoriety. Even on a smaller scale, not long after starting my podcast I began to get recognized in public. Then as the podcast grew, I got recognized even more. I was flattered by the love and support, but I still held true to my desire to fly under the radar.

When God revealed to me the changes to be made to my podcast, what frightened me more than anything was that I didn't feel like I was qualified to talk to people about God. I thought that in order to be used by God, you needed to have a seminary degree and to be some sort of bible scholar. I was none of that. I was and am just a regular woman who built a relationship with God for herself. I even struggled with writing this book because I thought, "Who am I to be talking to entrepreneurs about God?" I'm not a preacher, nor a millionaire. But that is exactly why God wanted to use me. He needed me to be unqualified so He could get the glory.

Like most people, I suffered from church hurt. I have gotten my feelings hurt in the house of God and made to feel like I was 'less than' on multiple occasions if I didn't fit the ideals of how a Christian should look or act. I have been in ministry meetings where people pushed their own needs more than the needs of those being served. I have seen countless religious leaders take empty approaches to service that only furthers the narrative of hypocrisy in the church. As I sought churches looking for a way to know God better, I was met with more of a handbook on what I shouldn't do more so than guidance on how to grow in my relationship with God. It wasn't until I distanced myself from a particular church home and focused on my relationship with God that I found what I was seeking.

What many churches get wrong is they try to chop down the tree without digging up the roots. Since the roots are still planted, the tree grows right back. They tell us to not sin, but don't bother to understand what our sins are rooted in. If we deal with the root of the sin, then we can really have a lasting impact on behavior. When I went to God for myself, I realized that He wanted my heart. When I gave Him my heart, I was able to correct behaviors. This time, I turned from sin because I wanted to please God, not because a religious leader condemned me for it. Pleasing God also meant coming to terms with His assignment for my life. I never wanted to become like those who hurt me which is one of the reasons I struggled with this new level of purpose God has given me. But I realize that it is in my authenticity, my rawness, and my inexperience with the formalities of religion, that I will be able to reach the people God wants me to reach. By not being qualified, I was a blank slate for God to use for his glory.

I find comfort in the story of David. David was the underdog. He was overlooked and kept himself busy tending to his sheep. When Samuel came to appoint one of Jesse's son's as king, David's father didn't even think to call him into the house. He gathered all of his other sons and left David in the field. It wasn't until Samuel asked if there were any more sons that Jesse called David in. This wasn't until after it was understood that none of the other sons were who God was going to appoint as king. David came into the house and God, through Samuel, appointed him as king. What I love the most about of this story is that David didn't need to do anything in his own strength. God didn't ask him for a degree, nor years of experience; He didn't check David's management capabilities. God chose David AND qualified him. After David was appointed as king, he went back to the field. He wasn't whisked away immediately to sit on the throne. There was a character building season he had to go through. Before he was able to kill Goliath, he had to kill a lion and bear in his own backyard first. Then with time and God building his character, he took the throne as king.

Imposter's syndrome is a perfect example that most of us don't feel qualified. Studies show that 70% of people suffer from imposter syndrome. By definition, imposter syndrome is a psychological pattern in which people doubt their accomplishments and have a persistent, often internalized fear of being exposed as a fraud. Maya Angelou is a notable figure who dealt with this pattern. She said, "I have written eleven books, but each time I think, 'Uh oh, they're going to find out now. I've run a game on everybody, and they're going to find me out." This shows that we all, at some point, don't feel qualified. But the medicine is and will always be resting in that God doesn't call the qualified, but He qualifies the called.

How awesome is it that God doesn't need you to try to qualify yourself? All you need to do is have a heart for Him and He will do the rest. If David would've had all of the experience needed to be a king, how would God get the glory for that? If you needed to have it all figured out on your own, how would God get the glory for that? Even in my life, as God is using me, the naysayers can say I am unqualified to talk to people about surrendering their business to God. I am not successful enough, I am not an ordained minister, I don't have a degree in divinity. The privilege I have of being chosen, is that I don't need any of that because God called me and will do a great work through me. He will do the same through you, if you make room for him.

Chapter 2: Make Room for God in Your Business

CHAPTER 2:

Make Room for God in Your Business

Have you ever felt any of these things? Check all that apply.

- o Unclear on what your purpose is
- o Afraid to start a business that's been on your mind/heart for years
- o You've hit a glass ceiling and don't know how to push through
- o You've started your business, but don't know when you'll ever be able to leave your full-time job
- o Wonder when your business will be able to function without you working non-stop
- o Understand the importance of God, but unsure how to surrender

If you checked any of these, it is time for you to make God a priority, so that you can be relieved of the pressure of making success happen in your own strength. When I first left Corporate America, I was afraid. I recognized God told me it was time for my leap of faith, but I didn't realize how difficult self-employment would be initially. I grew frustrated during the first few months because I was working non-stop with seemingly nothing to show for it. One day I came to a point of total frustration and asked God if He wanted me to leave my job, why was I not seeing results from all of the work I was doing on my business. He told me that in order for me to break the glass ceiling, He needed to be a part of my business for real. He told me my success was not going to happen without Him at the center of even the seemingly small details. God wants to not only give us the vision, but the blueprint. He wants us to involve him in every step of the process.

Clean House

But seek first the kingdom of God and His righteousness, and all these things shall be added to you. (Matt.6:33)

In order to make room for God, you have to do away with the old. The old is the way that you have always done things in your business. It's the way you think you should do business based on what you've learned from others or seen on social media. When God is the CEO, you no longer operate like everyone else. The bible does say to seek wise counsel, but in order for you to know which counsel to invest in, you still must seek God. Let's discuss some areas that most people tend to shut God out of.

Your Mouth

Usually around the fourth quarter of a year, people go into reflective mode. We start seeing the 'Top 9' photo collages of the year's accomplishments and proud moments. Then, around New Year's Eve, people begin discussing their goals or resolutions for the upcoming year. So naturally, as entrepreneurs, we do the same thing for our business. We compare our revenue to that of previous years, reflect on what did or didn't work in our businesses, and make new goals for the upcoming year.

In 2018, I started planning what to do with my brands a few months after I made God the CEO. I decided that instead of relying on what I knew, I was going to pray about it. As I prayed, God began to show me visions of how my year would be. The things He showed me scared me to death. Originally, I intended on my revenue goal being $150,000. But God said, "I am going to make you a millionaire this year and I will tell you how to do it." Not only did He tell me that, but I got confirmation from someone else as well. Even with all of my ambition, I could not rationalize how I was going to have this amazing, life changing year.

Now, the average person may have been super excited, but I was terrified. God pretty much told me that my million was contingent on my obedience. Talk about pressure! It scared me so much, I stopped praying about it because I just couldn't take it anymore. When I got back to setting my revenue goal, I wanted to write down the original $150,000 because it seemed more realistic to me than one million. When I picked up the marker to write it down, everything in me stopped me from writing down that number. Something inside me said, "Don't you dare." So instead, I wrote down one million dollars. Talk about a lot of zeroes! I realized in that moment that in order for me to tap into the next level God had for me, I needed to get in agreement with Him. The bible says, "Words kill, words give life; they're either poison or fruit—you choose" (*The Message, Prov. 18:21*).

After I decided to get aligned with what God said, even though I still didn't see the HOW, the devil provided me with many chances of speaking against it. I had a meeting with a couple of my entrepreneur friends to develop strategies on how we were going to meet our revenue goals for the following year. We discussed our marketing strategies, products and service offerings, then put our minds together to help each other come up with a plan that led to accomplishing our goals. The first thing we did was write down our revenue goals. Everyone else's goal was in the six-figure range which made it even easier for me to just go back to my six-figure number. Instead, I wrote down one million dollars once again.

I tried my best to plan with what I had, but God made it clear, He was going to direct my business to that figure. The only plan I really needed was to make sure I was always in position to hear from Him and be obedient. Shortly after that meeting, another entrepreneur friend of mine called me to inquire about my revenue goal for the upcoming year. He told me that he was checking up on all his entrepreneur friends to hold them accountable to their goals. I was annoyed because even though I made sure my words were in alignment with what God said, I was tired of talking about it. I also didn't want to hear unsolicited advice or opinions about it. Nevertheless, I told him, "I'm going to make a million and God is going to show me how to do it." He told me that was great and for me to reach that mark, I would need to make roughly $83,333.33 a month. As soon as he said that, I said a curse word in my head that starts with an 's' and ends with a 't'. My mouth definitely hadn't been all the way delivered at that point. All I could get out was 'yup'. My friend told me that he would check in with me monthly to see how I was doing with that number. When we got off of the phone, I remember asking God, "Please don't let him call me again about this." I wasn't quite comfortable yet because even though I was in agreement with God, I still had no clue where this million was coming from. I was just determined to not talk myself out of my own blessing.

A similar situation happened when a text thread comprised of another group of entrepreneur friends were discussing their goals. I said once again, "I'm going to make a million and God is going to show me how to do it." Even as I wrote this, I struggled with if I was going to say million or not, versus using a buffer like 'large number', just in case. In all transparency, I don't have anywhere near a million dollars at this point. However, I know what God said and confirmed. In my struggle with specifically writing million, I realize my hesitancy is rooted in skepticism. If I were to not write a million in this book, even though I am not verbally speaking, I am still going against what God said because my motives for withholding it, are rooted in a lack of faith. So here I am once again, writing in faith that, I will be a millionaire this year and God is going to tell me how to do it. Is your skepticism keeping you from getting into alignment with what God has planned for your life?

Take some time to think and pray about the following questions:

- o What has God told you that you're still skeptical about?
- o Are you in agreement with it?
- o Did He tell you that you're a successful entrepreneur, but every time someone asks, 'What do you do?' you tell them your title at your full-time job? Are you talking yourself out of your blessings?
- o Thankfully, none of my friends told me I was crazy (even though I would've completely understood if they did). I wasn't willing to talk myself out of my blessing. What do you need to start speaking out loud, even if you don't quite believe how it will manifest yet?

Your habits

One of my favorite books is called *The Power of Habit* by Charles Duhigg. The book debunks the myth that habits can be broken. Duhigg insists that instead of breaking habits we form new habits that replace the old. When you submit your business to God, you have to form new habits. This starts with what you do on a day to day basis.

I have a friend who is a Christian, wife, mother of four, entrepreneur, and a graduate student. Needless to say, she has a lot on her plate. In her testimony, she often discusses how there was a season in her life when things were out of order. She focused mainly on her business success, and her family life took a back seat. She describes that she had an extremely successful business, but that same success wasn't happening at home. She told me that for her to be able to, not only balance her responsibilities, but excel in each, she had to put things in the right order. That started with changing her habits and getting her priorities in line. The correct order is: God, family, business. When I first realized God needed to be my CEO, she began to serve as a mentor to me so I could fix my habits as well. I realized that even though I may have always said God was a priority in my life, my habits told a different story. I never read my bible because 'I didn't understand it'. I never spent time with God because 'there weren't enough hours in the day'. I barely went to the house of God because 'I couldn't wake up on time'. My commitment to my excuses showed my lack of commitment to receiving God's best for me. The same applied to my business.

None of the business gurus I looked up to talked about praying (in Jesus' name), prior to making big decisions. None of them seemed to be living their life for God beyond the bare minimum, yet all of them were still very successful. God had to show me though, not all successful people are saved. They also aren't living God's best for them, just because they are successful.

There is a difference between worldly success and kingdom success. That is why so many successful people battle with depression, commit suicide, or aren't happy. There is a level of peace that you operate in when you are successful in the kingdom. You can walk through the fire and know that you won't be burned when God is in control. When you are self-made, you have the added stress of always being the problem solver or the hero. But with God, you can always rest knowing that even when you are weak, He will be made strong in you. God showed me that MY path, meant I was going to have to make room for Him in my business NOW, or I would never get anywhere. For you to tap into God's best for you, you must:

- Spend time with him
- Read his word
- Be obedient

God will lead you to everything else. But by including those three bullet points in your daily life, you make room for God to be able to work in your life. I want to debunk some of the top habits/excuses that people have that keep them from making room for God:

1. **Time Management:** I learned that life isn't about balance, it's more so about priorities. If God is the number one priority in your life, for you to say you don't have time to spend with

Him, means all of the other things you have to do come before God. If you were in a relationship, and your partner spent all of his time with his friends and at work, then tells you he doesn't have any time to spend with you, you would be upset. You would look at him as if he values his friends or his job more than you.

God feels the same way. You value your business, your family, your friends, social media, and your ambitious, more than you value God. Take a look at all of the things you give your time to, is there anything you can remove to spend 15 minutes with God? If you woke up just 15 minutes earlier, you would be able to spend that time with God. If you stopped scrolling on social media and checking emails after you turned your alarm off, you could spend that time with God. Take a moment to reflect on what's on your plate currently. You can even take a piece of paper, draw a circle to symbolize a plate, and write down every single thing that takes up any of your time. What can you eliminate to make more room for God?

2. **Not seeking to understand the bible for ourselves:** When I first began my journey with God, reading the Bible was a struggle for me. I couldn't pronounce any of the names, I didn't understand the context, and overall the way it was written wasn't easy for me to comprehend. A friend told me about a Life Application Bible which is written in plain English and explains each verse in more detail so readers can easily understand. It also provides lots of context for you to understand what is going on in the stories. Additionally, I would make notes of scriptures referenced in sermons I enjoyed so I could go back and read them to comprehend them for myself. I would pray and ask God to speak to me through the scriptures so I could understand how they applied to my life. I didn't have time to continue to make excuses for why I wasn't reading the bible. My future is too important to only rely on what other people tell

me the bible says. We have such a bad habit of just believing what we hear without fact checking or asking questions. Especially in the age of social media. It is important for us as believers to break that habit and get in God's word for ourselves.

3. **Not wanting to be uncomfortable:** There is an old saying that says, "Life begins at the end of your comfort zone." For some reason, as soon as most of us get close to that line, we panic and are ready to run. One of my favorites scriptures is, " 'The Lord will perfect all things that concern you' (*New King James Version, Psalm 138:8*)." In order for God to perfect us, we have to be uncomfortable. In order for the potter to perfect His creation, it must be disfigured. In order for an ice sculpture to be perfected, the excess ice must be chopped off. Neither of these instances are comfortable, but they're for our good. In fact, discomfort is a sign that you are being perfected. Instead of looking at it as something to be afraid of, look at it as a sign that God is

moving in you. Pressure either bursts pipes, or makes diamonds. What will it do to you?

Chapter 3: He's the CEO You're the Manager

CHAPTER 3:

He's the CEO;

You're the Manager

After you make room for God, you understand what your role is and what it isn't. God is the CEO, you are just the manager of the vision He gave you. I didn't realize the distinction until God spoke to me during a sermon I was watching. It was so good I had about two full pages worth of notes. The sermon is called "Stride" by Pastor Mike Todd of *Transformation Church* in Tulsa, Oklahoma. That morning, I had been praying and asking God to show me what the real difference was of me being the CEO of my business and Him being the CEO. This sermon was a direct response to my prayer. Originally, I thought I was doing a good job of making God the CEO, but I learned that I was actually making God a consultant. I realized I would ask Him for direction only to consider what He said and not to obey it immediately. Sometimes I would apply it, other times I didn't. This sermon gave me the reprimand I needed to TRULY put God in charge. When you put God in charge of your business, you no longer occupy the driver's seat. You get out of the car, walk around, and get comfortable on the passengers side instead.

Imagine you and your significant other are driving to dinner. You are the driver and he is in the passenger seat. You are going out to eat but decide to take a way that you think will get you there faster. Since he doesn't understand why you are going that way, he fusses about your route. He then becomes a 'back seat driver' as we say. Instead of just fussing about the route you were taking, he decides to put his hands on the steering wheel and turn the car in the direction he believes you should be going. Not only does he get you off course by doing that, but you both could've been killed. It's the same thing when you don't make God the CEO of your business. You are the person in the passenger seat trying to take control of the wheel. Consequently, you drive your business into preventable trouble. You drive yourself and your business into financial hardship, failed marketing strategies, and overwhelm because you decided to put your hands on the steering wheel, versus letting God have His way.

CEO You vs. CEO God

Do you ever feel:

- Overwhelmed
- Constantly Tired
- Swamped in things to do in your business
- Like you're wasting your time praying for your business
- Like you keep hitting a glass ceiling and can't seem to break through
- You have no clue where to even start with the business idea you have
- Stressed about not being where you'd like to be

When you decided to start a business, it probably came from a passionate place. It might've been a gap you believed you could fill or God could've simply just put an idea on your heart and you created a business from it. When you form a business, you assume a leadership position, usually CEO or President. These roles require certain skills that we don't automatically acquire because we started a business. Take a look at the below job descriptions of CEO and president from *Workable* and *Indeed*:

Chief Executive Officer (CEO):

Chief Executive Officer or CEO supervises and controls all strategic and business aspects of the company. You will be the first in command in the company and responsible for giving the proper strategic direction, as well as creating a vision for success.

To thrive as a CEO you must be a prudent manager and an inspiring leader. The ideal candidate will have a business mindset, while being able to see the 'big picture' in a variety of settings. They will take actions to enhance the company's cash flow while keeping the human factor in perspective. The goal is to drive the company's development and guide it towards long-term success.

President:

The **president** is tasked with providing strong leadership for the company by working with the board and other executives to establish short and long-term goals, plans, and strategies. They are responsible for presiding over the entire workforce and they will manage budgets to make sure resources are allocated properly. The president will make sure departments meet their individual goals and are responsible for overall accountability to shareholders and the general public. They will encourage business investment from the community and act as the public face of the company. In addition, the person in the role of president must have an entrepreneurial mindset and adapt quickly to changes in the marketplace.

Do you feel you're qualified to take on those responsibilities? Most likely not. Because of this, you may think you have to take classes, hire coaches, get degrees, etc., to become good at the 'business' of your company. You may even allow this to prevent you from starting your business altogether.

Most of the time, God will use those who don't have the qualifications so He can get the glory for the success. Because of this, we must not make decisions based on our own perceived limitations and definitely must not let our limitations stop us. When God is the CEO, there are no limitations. I am not saying don't hire coaches, take classes, or get degrees. I am saying if you are to do those things, do so because God told you to, not because you feel like you need to in order to be successful. We must qualify every decision we make in our business. If God is not in the decision-making process, then it is clear that we are the CEO and He isn't. If God put a vision inside you, and you let fear stop you from seeing it out, you are still being disobedient. Procrastination is still disobedience. God doesn't want you to be average, normal, or regular. He created you to be extraordinary, so you must give birth to the ideas He has impregnated you with, using His guidance, even when you aren't qualified.

You: Outwork everybody
God: Out pray everybody

1 John 5:14-15 New International Version (*NIV*)
[14] This is the confidence we have in approaching God: that if we ask anything according to his will, he hears us. [15] And if we know that he hears us—whatever we ask—we know that we have what we asked of him.

One of my favorite quotes used to be: "You have to work as if someone else is working 24-hours a day to take it all away from you," by Marc Cuban. Whenever I got tired or grew weary in my entrepreneurial journey, thinking of this quote kept me working. In my mind, I would have to outwork everybody to be successful. As my relationship with God grew, I learned that there is a privilege I have with Him being the CEO. That privilege is even IF someone is working 24-hours a day to take it all away from me, my God goes ahead of me and makes crooked paths straight. While yes, I must still have a strong work ethic, my work looks a little different than most. Instead of spending day and night working just in/on the businesses, I have to develop a strong prayer life. I have to learn to hear God's voice and be obedient to everything he tells me to do, even when it is uncomfortable. I have to consistently surrender my plans and objectives in order to carry out the vision God has placed inside of me. So yes, while I outwork everybody, that 'work' now includes God. The problem is, your favorite success story isn't telling you these things. If you spend three hours in your prayer closet seeking God on behalf of a deal you have on the table, it may be perceived as you sleeping on the job. But When God is your CEO, this is included in your 'work'. If these things don't sound like they're necessary or important to you, this is a key sign you are your own CEO, not God.

When I first became an entrepreneur, I often felt the exact same way. There were times where it was only Wednesday, but I was burnt out, relying on coffee to even get out of the bed. Overworking yourself is a sign that you don't trust God to take you where you're going. When God is the CEO, you don't have to over exert yourself anymore. You just have to do what He says and He will take care of everything else for you. Imagine having somebody who no one even sees, out there working 24-hours a day for things to work out for your good; Out there leveling the playing field of people who you think are far beyond you. Turning the people you admire into your contemporaries. That is what God does. Your success is a part of His plan and He will make it happen for you, you just have to trust Him. It gives me such a boost of confidence and peace that I am not doing things on my own. It gives me authority to silence my inner hustler, because my God is in control and He always wins.

You: Hire a coach/mentor
God: Qualify who Pours into You

When you're the CEO of your business, you tend to disregard the source of the people who are teaching you. You may see someone who has written multiple New York Times Best-selling books and because you would like to accomplish that as well, you hire them as a coach. But the only qualifier you considered is their success and not their character. You didn't take a moment to determine who their source is. Then, you end up learning from somebody who doesn't even believe in what or who you believe in. The devil will use your ambition to open up doors for people to destroy you. Then, because you're not in tune with God, your own desires end up driving your decision making, causing you to use limited judgement. The bible says we are to seek wise counsel. Wisdom is rooted in the word of God, so the person you are positioning yourself to be a student under must have wisdom rooted in God.

I'm at a place where I don't want to learn from anyone who doesn't have a relationship with God. If they don't have a foundation of God in their business, we don't have any business together. I need to be able to know that you can hear from God enough to a point where if He needs to interject in our session, you're sensitive to His voice. I need to know that if you have plans to talk to me about sales that day, but God says, "No talk to her about her habits," you can negate your plans and be obedient to God's word. At the very least, I need to know that if I ask you to pray for me, we are praying to the same God.

A spiritual foundation is necessary for anyone who is involved with influencing the vision God has given me. It is easiest to kill a vision in its infancy stages, so we must protect our 'baby' at all costs. When you have God as the CEO of your business, you must have a level of discernment. In order for someone to pour into you in any way, they have to be filled with something. If I had two empty water glasses and I tried to pour from one to the other, nothing would come out because nothing is there. On the contrary, if I had one glass full of water and the other full of oil and I pour that oil into the water glass, I have now tainted what was once pure. This is why it is important to pay particular attention to who/what is pouring into who you allow to pour into you.

When God is your CEO, the devil is like the competitor who continuously tries to shut your business down. He pays attention to everything you do, every stride you make, and strategically tries to kill, steal, and destroy everything you've worked for. A mistake a lot of us make is where we underestimate how well the enemy knows us and how intentional he is about destroying us. He will send a dream-killer in the form of that business coach you admire and have been saving up to work with. It may be a dream-killer in the form of that opportunity you have been believing in God for. Don't ever disregard the source of whoever is teaching you.

You: I'm a hustler
God: My timing is perfect

Habakkuk 2:3 New Living Translation (*NLT*)
[3] This vision is for a future time.
It describes the end, and it will be fulfilled.
If it seems slow in coming, wait patiently,
for it will surely take place.
It will not be delayed.

I have never been a huge fan of the word 'hustle'. Whenever I thought about a hustler or observed people who referred to themselves as hustlers, it never seemed organized or secure. I've never met a hustler with longevity. According to the dictionary, the verb tense of to hustle is "to force or to move hurriedly or unceremoniously in the specified direction or to obtain by forceful action." I want to be clear that my opinion is based on what I've seen of hustlers and what the dictionary definition is. You may define hustle in another way that is more personal to you, which is fine. But for the sake of my point here, we are discussing this in the context of its standard definition.

Even though I never identified myself as a hustler, I have always had hustler habits. It wasn't until about a year ago that I got the revelation that hustling is a sign that God is not your CEO and you are attempting to build His vision in your own strength. Forced and hurried are the key words in the definition of hustle. The noun version is "busy movement and activity, a fraud, or a swindle." Most of us use hustle in the sense that we're forcing, we're busy, we're moving hurriedly in a certain direction which is whatever level of success we're working towards. Whenever I think of hustlers, I also think of drug dealers. They move hurriedly because they're doing something illegal and they don't want to go to jail. For the rest of us, we are in a hurry because we feel if we are moving slowly, we will miss our opportunities or never achieve success. This was my same mindset, feeling like I had to hustle because if I didn't hustle, I wasn't going to reach my goals. I didn't understand that the space between where we are and where we want to be is the most important part of the journey. Hustling makes us rush through the character building process. Then whenever we do reach the success we have been hustling for, we lose it, or we mishandle it because we didn't embrace the preparation season. Did you know that God already promised you success? It isn't a matter of if – it is a matter of when. The in-between is where you are getting prepared. So embrace and see the beautiful opportunities in the character building season. In the aforementioned sermon by Pastor Mike Todd, he said, "Anything that you do fast, causes damage." When I heard that, I thought about how a couple months ago I got into a minor car accident. I came out of the gas station into the lane at no more than five miles per hour and I hit the back of another car. Since I was moving so slowly, I had no structural damage to my car. What's also important in this story is the reason I was going so slow – I wasn't in a rush. I wasn't in a rush because I was confident that my destination would be there when I got there. It wasn't going to look different if I sped up; it wasn't going to be better because I rushed; it was going to be exactly the same. It wasn't going to stop being my destination if someone got there before me. There were no contingencies that if I out drove everybody, somehow my arrival would be more special. It was for me, and it wasn't going to stop being my destination.

On the contrary, if I were to have been speeding, I would've caused so much stress and damage for myself. I would have wrecked my car and someone else's car, and possibly ended up hurt. With that would've come medical bills, increased insurance, and a host of other problems all because I was rushing and not operating at a steady pace – God's pace. The same applies to business: anything you do fast causes damage. If you are rushing to put out a book, you may skip necessary steps to put out a product that is of great quality. The book will be published with typos, grammatical errors, and it will lack information because no time was taken for quality control. In my consulting work, I have seen lots of entrepreneurs rush in the very beginning stages of business. They are so quick to post on social media and talk about being an entrepreneur, they put up websites and products for sale without ever legally forming a business. Hustling can cause you to focus so much on the money or the next thing, that quality control is swept under the rug. Surrendering your business to God, means surrendering to His timing as well.

Taming your inner hustler is definitely easier said than done. Some people naturally move at a fast pace, so it may be difficult to slow down to get on pace with God's timing. This is where discipline and creating new habits come into play.

Practical ways to ensure you are keeping your inner hustler in check and staying on pace with God:

1. Start your day with God
2. Pray about everything and WAIT to hear from God before you act
3. Don't make decisions on the spot
4. Read your bible consistently
5. Seek wise counsel (that also have a relationship with God)

You: I'm giving my business my all
God: Excellence can't be Compartmentalized

God is excellence. Since the bible says we are made in his image, that means we are to be excellent as well. The problem is, many of us never truly master excellence in all areas of our lives. Being excellent in business, and mediocre in health is not acceptable. Having a successful business and a failing marriage is unacceptable. It's important to note that excellence is not perfection. Instead, it is the commitment to consistently being outstanding in all areas of life. If you find yourself in a season where you are laser focused in your business and everything else seems to be stagnant, you are doing yourself and God a disservice.

My father and I have very similar personalities. He is a very blunt and straight forward man, who never sugar coats anything he has to say. One day he told me I needed to lose weight. His rationale was, I can't put myself in a position to help or inspire people and be overweight. While it was harsh, at the root of what he was saying was a valid point. How could I stand on stages and speak on podcasts about excellence and living your best life while obviously neglecting my health. I was so focused on fulfilling the vision, I wasn't taking care of my temple. It showed that there was an area in my life I was undisciplined in. That isn't excellence.

That lesson stuck with me because I strive to live a life of excellence which encompasses all areas. When I first became an entrepreneur, I was not taking care of myself. I was not working out, I sat in front of my computer all the time, I was not eating right, and gained a lot of weight. I was so focused on being an entrepreneur, I neglected my own health. What's worse is that I was creating negative habits that would only hurt me in the long haul. African Americans are dying young at alarming rates because of heart disease, diabetes, and other preventable illnesses. If I would have kept up those habits, I would be a successful entrepreneur who did not live to enjoy my success. I quickly realized I couldn't focus so much on my business success that I was lacking everywhere else. What's the good of having a business or entrepreneurial success if you don't love yourself? What good is that success if your emotional or mental health is suffering or if your family is falling apart?

This became even more real for me when I got engaged. I have not had the best examples of a successful marriage in my life, so I always knew that when my time came, I wanted to have a healthy marriage. After I said yes, somewhere in the midst of engagement bliss, I realized I needed to now take the relationship a lot more seriously. This was no longer my boyfriend who I loved so much. He was now going to be my husband. I was going to become one with this person to fulfill God's purpose with him. I wasn't thinking as much about a big wedding or pretty dresses as I was about legacy. With that, my fiancé' and I had to talk about what our marriage was going to be and put controls in place to protect our union. I had to realize there were some things within myself that couldn't get taken into a marriage.

I prayed and asked God to send me a husband. The time to prepare for that commitment to be married was now in place. At the same time though, I still had my business and my assignment that wasn't going to lack either. Because I knew even if I had the greatest marriage in the world, I would never be happy without my businesses being successful and my purpose being fulfilled. So in the engagement season, I had to become excellent in my priorities to keep any area from lacking.

I've learned that a lot of people pray and seek God to expand their territory or improve their current circumstances, but never ask God to show them how they can master the level where they currently are. If you don't know how to manage the money you have, you will mismanage your financial increase as well. We have to be good stewards where we are while we wait for God to promote us. His timing won't change, so we must shift our focus to preparing ourselves for the things we are asking Him for.

I found myself recently asking God for a lot. I was asking for an increase financially, new opportunities, material things, etc. I was asking for so much, I began getting on my own nerves. I figured that because I was being obedient and serving God, I could just ask Him for things and get them when I wanted to. I was acting like a spoiled brat with God. When I wasn't seeing my prayers answered as quickly as I wanted them to and I was getting frustrated with God, I realized I was the problem. I needed to change my perspective. I needed to stop focusing on what I wanted to get, and become excellent in what I already had. I made a list of everything I was believing in God for, then compared that to my current circumstances and found ways to be more excellent in what I had.

For example, I wrote in my prayer journal that I wanted to purchase my first home in an affluent area in Washington, D.C. Then, I looked at where I currently lived and found ways to be excellent with that place. I realized that I couldn't ask God for a 8,000 square foot house if I wasn't taking care of my 800 square foot apartment. I couldn't believe in God for my dream vehicle, a Porsche Panamera, when I was not taking care of my Nissan Sentra. I couldn't ask God to expand my territory and bless me with influence if I was not taking care of my well-being. If I was not taking care of my health, I wouldn't live long enough to enjoy His blessings.

What are some ways that you can be excellent with what you have now, while you are believing in God for more?

You: I've gotten myself this far

God: I know what's best for you

_____

Being 'self-made' is the biggest lie in the world. We give ourselves too much credit to think that what we are able to produce in our own strength even compares to what God can do through us.

Take a look at your exes and relationship choices. That is a sign that we don't always know what's best for us. Imagine if that business idea you've been working so hard toward wasn't even the vision God had for you? In today's age, with social media, it is easy to get caught up in comparisons, thinking we should do something because we see someone else being successful at it. Or we may think we shouldn't do the thing God has placed inside of us because 'everyone' is doing it.

There are too many factors that shape our decision making and we don't always know what's best. That's why it is important to seek God in all things because He already knows your end from your beginning. He doesn't care how many people own beauty salons; He has something special for yours. He doesn't care that no one has done what you're trying to do before; He chose you to be the pioneer and break barriers. He doesn't care that no one in your family is an entrepreneur; He wanted you to be the first, so those coming after you can be exposed to entrepreneurship.

We constantly have to check with God to make sure that what we're doing is the right thing; it is vital to keep us from pursuing someone else's purpose for ourselves and wondering why it's not working out. The reason most of us don't know what's for us and what isn't is because God isn't included in the planning process. Instead, we try to do our own thing and when it doesn't work out, we ask Him to fix our mess. You put your hands on the steering wheel and turned it in the wrong direction because you thought that's where you were supposed to go only to end up in the wrong place. Consequently, wasting time, energy, money, sweat, and tears. God is such a gentleman He will still give us grace and redirect us back to His path. But why go through that if you don't have to?

Chapter 4: How to Make God the CEO

CHAPTER 4:

How to Make God the CEO

The STEEP System

In my experience with making God the CEO of my business, there have been four factors that were pivotal in learning how to let God lead me. I like to call it the STEEP System:

1. Surrender
2. Trust
3. Eliminate Excuses
4. Prayer

Let's dive into what each of these mean and how they will ultimately benefit you.

Surrender + Trust

By definition, to surrender means to submit to an authority. Submission is often difficult because it requires forfeiting our own desires, even when our pride doesn't want us to. Submission to God is difficult because it requires you to give up control to a force you can't physically see. This is why surrendering will only really work if you have full faith in God and trust Him. If not, you will find yourself consistently trying to take back control of what you submitted to Him. The pre-requisite to making God the CEO of your business is to have faith and trust that He can do all things. Most importantly, He can do all things better than you.

I am not the type of person who is eagerly willing to trust or submit. That didn't change when it came to my spiritual life. It was difficult for me to surrender my business and trust God because I thought my work ethic and intelligence would be able to get me as far as I wanted to go. I know this may be true for you as well. You may say that you surrender and trust God, but your actions show that you often revert back to your old ways of trying to do things in your own strength. I was the same way. For that reason, I had to build trust with God from the ground up and learn how to surrender by taking things one day at a time.

So don't worry about tomorrow, for tomorrow will
bring its own worries. Today's trouble is enough for
today.
– Matthew 6:34 NLT

I had to make surrendering to God a habit, and document the results to help build up my trust. This meant that whenever God answered a prayer I documented it; Whenever I received a blessing I documented it; Whenever I got a word from God I documented it. By documenting the results of surrendering, I was able to trust God more and more. When you're doing something new, it is not a habit yet, but rather it's an isolated incident. I wanted to make seeking God second nature to me. While I know the importance of your relationship with God not being routine, I needed a routine in the beginning so that I could remain consistent. I had to train my flesh to seek God and not just go with my natural reaction. I wanted Godly instincts. In order for me to do that, I began to start my day every day with God.

I also had to be honest with God. In my prayer time, I asked God to light a fire for Him inside of me. My entire life, I had been consistently inconsistent in my relationship with God. I would be super pumped up for a few months, then fall off. I would get pumped up again for another few months, then fall off for years. I knew I could not continue that pattern, especially with my business and future on the line. Asking God to light a fire on the inside of me was my prayer to end my previous patterns. I wanted to be passionate about pleasing God, just as I was passionate about being a successful entrepreneur. If I'm being honest, I wasn't passionate about praying every day, reading the bible, or even about making God the CEO of my business. If I was, I would've already been committed to it. Instead, I was more passionate about my ambition and success, which is why I worked so hard every day. God answered my prayer, and I have been on fire for Him ever since.

If you find yourself struggling to surrender, start by being honest with God and yourself. He knows the truth anyway. Lay all the cards out on the table. Tell Him about the hurt you have experienced in church that has caused you to rebel against your faith. Tell Him that you don't know how to hear His voice yet, so you aren't even sure if you're doing the right thing. Tell Him that you just want to be sure that He's real. There is nothing wrong with being vulnerable with God. Remember, He already knows these things. It's when you are able to truly be vulnerable, and God answers your prayers, that you will be able to trust and surrender.

Eliminating Excuses

George Washington Carver said that 99% of failures come from people who make a habit out of making excuses. If you allow yourself to fall into the rabbit hole of excuses, the enemy will lead you to 100+ reasons why you can't accomplish your goal. Or bombard your mind with a ton of 'What if?' scenarios to talk you out of surrendering to God. What if this doesn't work? What if you still fail? What if God lets you down? What if you don't make any money? I would even dare to ask you, "What if you keep doing what you've been doing?" The same method that keeps you busy versus being productive, stressed instead of having joy and peace, or side hustling instead of living in your purpose full-time? It is time to eliminate all excuses and commit to aligning yourself with the will of God. He will never leave you nor forsake you.

Prayer

Therefore, I tell you, whatever you ask for in prayer, believe that you have received it, and it will be yours. - *Mark 11:24*

War Room

One morning I woke up tired and uninspired, with a to-do list that seemed to never end. It was not too long after I left my full-time job to pursue entrepreneurship full-time. I had money going out every day and no money coming in from my business. I was growing more and more frustrated as the days went by. That particular morning as I was reviewing the things I had to do that day, I heard God tell me to watch the movie, *War Room*. I was annoyed at the thought because watching a movie didn't seem like a productive thing to do when I wasn't making any money. I decided to be obedient and watch the movie. I quickly understood the main point of the movie and just assumed that God wanted me to pray more. I took a mental note of the message and went on about my day. After watching the movie, I went to my local library to check out some business books. As I was browsing in the marketing section, I saw a book that was out of place and oddly directly facing me. It was the book *Fervent* by Priscilla Shirer. I didn't know what the word fervent meant, so I was going to just look past the book until I saw a sticker on it that said, 'from the movie War Room'. I instantly knew that God was trying to show me something. I immediately checked out the book and went straight home to read it. That book totally transformed my relationship with God.

The movie planted the seed of the power of prayer, but that book watered it. So much has grown from me learning how to pray strategically. I created a war room in my closet where I took every single thing to God in prayer in the format that was described in that book. I also wrote down all of my prayers and began to record when they were answered. By developing a strong prayer life, my relationship began to grow, my business grew substantially, and I was finally able to reap the benefits of making God the CEO. If you are struggling with developing a prayer life, I suggest you read the book as well and apply the very practical steps Shirer provides in the book. You cannot make God the CEO of your business without prayer and sensitivity to His voice.

Chapter 5: When Success Becomes an Idol

CHAPTER 5:

When Success Becomes an Idol

Studies show that there is a direct link between social media and mood disorders. I believe that social media encourages people to put false expectations and unreasonable timelines on their own achievements. When you are working hard to get a degree or start a business in which you can ultimately be successful, scrolling on your timeline to see someone who doesn't seem to be working as hard to succeed can take a toll on you. Especially in today's world where it seems all you have to do is show your body or be funny and you have the cheat code to success. We are constantly bombarded with the highlight reel of people's lives. We see everyone with designer clothes, shoes, cars, etc., and it subconsciously makes us feel as if we aren't accomplishing anything if we don't have those things to show as well.

Have you fallen into the comparison game? Are you comparing your life to those you see online? I have fallen victim to it myself. Comparison robs you of the opportunity to appreciate the blessings you currently have. This is why it is important to not only limit social media use, but define what success means to you and have controls in place to make sure you stay on track and smell the roses along the way.

What does success mean to you?

Take a moment to think about what success means to you. Success can only be defined by your individual desires. When I used to think about what success meant to me, I thought I had it all figured out. Success to me meant the freedom of my time, never worrying about money, and doing something in the world that outlived me. I didn't want to be confined to the cubicle life. I am not saying there is anything wrong with it. But for me, I had to change who I was at work. I had to 'code switch' as we call it in the black community, to play the game in order to get ahead. I always felt that if I needed to become someone else in order to be successful, that particular type of success was not for me.

I also wanted the freedom from worrying about money. Money is the root of all evil and when people magnify it, they often do either illegal or immoral things to obtain it. I didn't want to ever have to think about not having enough money. I wanted to be free from checking a price tag before I bought something. I desired to be able to put my bills on auto-pay without being concerned about whether the payment would go through. I didn't want to fall victim to the poverty mindset that keeps so many of us in a mental prison.

Lastly, I wanted my life to mean something. When the Lord calls me home, I want to leave something on this earth that my grandchildren and the world can continue to use to grow. I want to know that because of me and my impact, the world is a better place.

It wasn't until a few months ago that I realized my definition of success was all wrong. God began to tell me I needed to study the book of Jeremiah. This book is not the easiest to understand or comprehend because not only is it a very long book, but it isn't written in chronological order. This makes it very difficult to follow. So instead of just reading it, I decided to purchase a bible study on it instead. I bought a six-week bible study that breaks down the different themes of the book. As I went through the study, I realized that God considered Jeremiah successful. He was a prophet and his main job was to deliver messages to the people of Israel that worshipping false idols would cause their destruction. He was assigned to communicate the wrath of God to the people. Jeremiah was obedient to everything God told him to do despite any circumstance. Because the people were not a fan of his messages, they tried to kill him, they talked about him, and they treated him horribly. He often got frustrated with the lack of reception to God's word and couldn't understand why God wanted him to continue speaking.

Nevertheless, Jeremiah was still obedient and spoke every word God gave him. This was success in God's eyes. Success is pleasing God, not necessarily the concept of success that you had for your life. Now, with that, God will give us the desires of our heart; He will bless us tremendously because He knows our heart, but those blessings have a place. And that place will always be second to pleasing God. When I came to this realization in my bible study, I realized why God told me to study Jeremiah. I was too consumed with my idea of success. I put too much stock in my ambition and my goals, instead of having peace pleasing God. We naturally and subconsciously magnify things we focus on. The reason I was so anxious about things I believed God for is because I put too much value in it. Pleasing God is not a sexy Instagram post. Pleasing God doesn't win us awards or accolades from people. But it is success.

I didn't realize my ambitions had become my idol. I thought I was supposed to wake up every day and outwork everybody for my goals. I thought entrepreneurship was about the grind and reaping the rewards of it. I wasn't wrong, but I put these things on too high of a pedestal. I put these things before God. It's very easy for us all to allow our ambition and social media to make success an idol, so we have to be intentional about making sure it is secondary to God.

Chapter 6:
Identity Crisis

CHAPTER 6:

Identity Crisis

When I was in college, I had a professor deviate from her usual lesson when she asked us to write down and answer three questions:

- Who am I?
- Am I really who I say I am?
- Am I all I ought to be?

 For some reason, these three questions have continued to stick with me through the years. She used these as the basis to teach us about the 'Self Actualization Theory' by Abraham Maslow. Maslow had created this hierarchy of needs that resembled the food pyramid. Self-actualization means to achieve one's full potential. According to Maslow, in order for us to reach this level, we must have physiological, safety, belongingness, love, and esteem needs met first. I was fascinated by this theory because I wanted to reach my full potential, but based on my answer to the first three questions, I had a lot of work to do. This lesson sparked something in me to be intentional about discovering who I am. Not in a sense of exploring with boys, drugs, or any self-deprecating behavior, but figuring out how to have a positive answer to those three questions. I wanted to reach the top of Maslow's pyramid of self-actualization.

Who am I?

Growing up, I was sort of a trouble maker. From as early as I can remember, spankings, time-outs, punishment, yelling, and any other type of discipline you can think of was a part of my norm. I didn't like following the rules and I wanted things to always go my way. In school, I was always bored and looked for ways to occupy my time. Whether they were good or bad things didn't matter to me. This led to mischievous behavior which earned me the nick name 'Tatum Tantrum' from my teachers. My boredom was rooted in the fact that I was so naturally smart and gifted. In a few minutes, I understood what would take teachers hours to explain to other students. I was often impatient and frustrated that I had to still sit there all day, whether I understood the concepts or not. Since I was too young to effectively decode and communicate my emotions, anger was the easiest way to let out my frustration. One of my family's favorite stories to tell is how I was almost suspended in kindergarten because I threw my shoe at another student. I know, crazy. My mom had to come to the school and beg the principal to give me another chance and not expel me for my behavior.

Looking back, my ability to pick up on things quickly is a major reason why I would never be comfortable in a traditional job. Corporate America judges experience and skill by years of performing certain tasks, rather than competency or the ability to actually do it well. So, if Suzie has 3-5 years of project management experience, and I have one, but can manage a project so well it saves everyone involved time and money, Suzie will always get called for an interview before me. This concept that time equates competency is flawed to me. What if Suzie delegated all her work or only performed the bare minimum requirements for 3 - 5 years?

I felt the same way as a young child. If I could sit in the classroom for a couple of hours, retain the information, and pass the tests, why did I need to stay the whole day? I had a first-grade teacher named Ms. Rick who was the only teacher who understood why I was acting out. She was an older woman, very sweet, and had a level of patience with me that many other adults didn't have. She noticed how quickly I caught on to concepts and how much more advanced I was than the other students. I remember her suggesting to my mother one day that it may be a good idea for me to skip a grade so I could be more challenged in the classroom. I don't remember my mother's reaction, but I didn't skip a grade so I assume the answer was no.

It made me feel good about myself that Ms. Rick took the time to understand me and make the recommendation. It seemed that I was finally understood beyond the crazy, angry little girl flipping tables. Yes, I really did flip tables. As I got older, I no longer threw tantrums, but that feeling of being misunderstood never went away; neither did the desire to be understood and accepted.

At home, I lived with my mother, my father, and my older brother, Tyrell. My sister Jalysa didn't live in the house with us but would spend weekends with us occasionally. My mother worked at Children's Hospital and my father was a detective for the Washington D.C. Police Department. From the outside looking in, we were a pretty normal, middle class, blended family living in the suburbs of Fort Washington, Maryland just outside of Washington, D.C.

My family dynamic was another contributor to my nagging feeling of being misunderstood. My brother is five years older than me. My mother had him from a previous relationship, so we don't have the same father. Since my mother had Tyrell at 18, instead of going to college after high school, she decided to enter the workforce to provide for them. From my understanding, when my parents met, my brother's father was not involved in his life and my father took on the responsibility of raising him with my mother. My sister and I are half siblings as well, with the same father and different mothers. While this family dynamic may not be traditional to the societal expectation of two people being married before having children together, it was my normal. And I love my siblings more than anything.

Up until middle school, I spent the majority of my time with my father since my mother worked during the day and my father worked at night. At that age, I was very fond of my father and would even dare call myself a 'daddy's girl'. He gave me whatever I wanted and didn't fight me when I faked sick on days I didn't want to go to school. My father always understood my point of view, as he and I have very similar personalities. With him, I felt like I could always communicate and rationalize how I felt, even if I was wrong, and he would listen. Even when I was in trouble and getting punished, he still listened; I appreciated that. Talking to him gave me that same feeling I got when Ms. Rick saw me as gifted instead of angry: understood. This is why as years went on, and my relationship with my father got strained, it hit me very hard.

Around middle school, my mother got involved with a network marketing company. She rose to the top of the ranks in the company and became a highly respected and sought-after speaker and trainer in the organization. She was quickly able to retire from her job at the hospital and be in business for herself full-time. This was my first exposure to the concept of entrepreneurship. Despite my desire at that age to have my mother more physically present, that exposure to the entrepreneurial lifestyle showed me it was possible for me to one day wake up every morning and do what I love.

Eventually, my father left his job at the police department as well and began to work with my mother full-time. As their organization grew and more money was made, we were living an amazing life from the outside looking in. We had built a house from the ground up and had multiple luxury vehicles. I had lavish birthdays, and every material thing I could ask for. Unfortunately, I learned then that money doesn't buy happiness. It was also during this time that my parents' relationship began to change. At least this is when I was able to realize it. There was a lot more arguing, a lot more tension in the house, and a lot less love and laughter.

During my teenage years, I endured a lot of trauma that led to baggage and brokenness I tried to brush under the table even into my adult years. For years, I suffered from depression, anxiety, and self-sabotaging behavior. I was taught early 'what happens in this house stays in this house', which meant I learned young how to hide behind a fake smile and the words, "I'm Fine."

When my professor asked us those three questions, I realized I didn't know who I was. I knew I was smart and gifted; but my brokenness, inability to truly be vulnerable, and my desire to be understood prevented me from reaching my full potential. My identity up until that point had been wrapped in my upbringing. I had no idea where to start to get to know who I really was, despite what I had been through.

Who does God say I am?

After that class I had a bit of a moment in my dorm room. I was looking in the mirror frustrated because I wanted to reach my full potential, but I was so lost as to who I was. I didn't have a strong relationship with God at the time, but I was a believer. I prayed and asked God to show me who I was. I wanted to do more than just go to school and work. I wanted to have purpose. At the time, I didn't have the knowledge to comprehend what I was hearing from God. But I do remember as I stared at myself in the mirror, I began to see a glow. Instead of just me looking at my reflection, I felt like God was with me letting me know I was special. It was now only a matter of turning my pain into something positive. It was time to remove the mask of, "I'm fine," that I wore so well and use my experiences and vulnerability to help others.

First, I began a blog on my campus called 'Dear Regina…'. Since vulnerability was new to me and not something that came easy, I found that writing blogs in the form of letters allowed me to speak as if I was talking to someone I knew, instead of just opening up completely to strangers. I found that Regina was Latin for 'queen'. I wanted to write to the queen in me, as well as, the queen in other young women to help navigate the growing pains of life.

My blog quickly caught on and became very popular. My blog provided healing for me. It allowed me to discuss important topics that had kept me in bondage up until that point, while also inspiring others. Shortly after, I started volunteering and doing more mentoring on and around my campus. Through my blog and community service, I found purpose. I was able to see that my life meant something. My brokenness didn't define me. Instead, it empowered me. It gave me the wisdom to connect with and encourage others. After graduation, I continued to volunteer with youth programs and eventually started one of my own. I began to see myself in a new light based on the difference I was making in the lives of others.

Since I have transitioned to make God the CEO of my business, it was like I was blessed with a new pair of lenses to see myself the way He sees me. I have always known I was special, but through growing in God, I have learned that my perception of who I am is minuscule compared to who God says I am. God has revealed things about my life that I couldn't begin to imagine myself. I even see the fruit in what He is doing in my life right now. God has shown me that my voice is powerful. To have a podcast reaching so many all over the world is the fruit of that; To meet people who listen to my show when I travel and hear all of the positive, heartwarming things they say about how I have impacted them, is the fruit of what God showed me.

As I write this book I am nervous, yet so excited because I know that through my obedience, this book is going to reach the masses and impact people in a way I never could have done on the small scale I had in mind. God's best always supersedes our perception of what's best. God knew us before we were even formed in our mother's womb. He called us and set us apart before birth. We just need to seek Him to learn what we truly are. Too many times, we allow circumstances, past hurts, or our upbringing to define who we are. Those things may be a part of us but ultimately, we are who God says we are. Our identity is and will always be in Christ.

A prayer for new lenses

I would have failed you if I completed this chapter without urging you to seek God on behalf of who you are. It's okay if you're like me and don't really know what your life means. It's okay to still be searching and discovering your purpose. It's okay to still be broken or have pain from something that has happened to you. But now that you are able to identify these things, it is your responsibility to go to God and begin to heal. It's up to you to learn about who you are in Christ and seek wisdom from The Source on what your assignment is here on Earth. If you have found yourself in an identity crisis, pray and ask God for a new pair of lenses to see yourself the way He sees you. In addition to praying for new lenses, I have included a few scripture references below that show you who you are in Christ. Utilize them in your prayers and keep them at the forefront of your mind when the enemy tries to tell you that you're less than or your circumstances don't reflect what they say. It is important that despite what you see, you stand on (and speak to) what you know.

Scripture references:

- **Genesis 1:27** - So God created human beings in his own image. In the image of God he created them; male and female he created them.

- **Jeremiah 1:5** - I knew you before I formed you in your mother's womb. Before you were born I set you apart and appointed you as my prophet to the nations.

- **1 Peter 2:9** - But you are not like that, for you are a chosen people. You are royal priests, a holy nation, God's very own possession. As a result, you can show others the goodness of God, for he called you out of the darkness into his wonderful light.

- **2 Corinthians 5:17** - Therefore, if anyone is in Christ, he is a new creation. The old has passed away; behold, the new has come.

- **Ephesians 2:10** - For we are God's masterpiece, created to do good works which God prepared in advance for us to do

Chapter 7:

Fasting

CHAPTER 7:

Fasting

There was a period God would always speak to me through a close friend of mine as I was learning to hear His voice for myself. I had been believing in God for a few things and wasn't seeing the answers to my prayers. I was getting frustrated because up until that point, God had been very consistent with answering my prayers. It seemed as if when it came to the bigger decisions I was facing, I wasn't hearing from Him or seeing any action. I had not talked to my friend at all about how I was feeling, I had just written it down in my journal.

One day out of nowhere, this friend texted me 'Mark 9:29' and told me the Lord wants me to fast from 6 a.m. – 6 p.m. from all food. I called and began to ask her about fasting. Up until that point, I had been to churches who did group fasts, I had heard of things like the Daniel Fast, but I had never fasted for myself. I began to think about why God wanted me to fast from food instead of something else like maybe social media or television. I realized that food was the one thing I felt like I couldn't fast from. Not eating anything from 6 a.m. - 6 p.m. seemed impossible, especially if I was awake for that entire time. This is why I knew it was food I needed to fast from. Anything I felt so strongly against giving up was exactly what I needed to sacrifice for God.

My friend gave me some wisdom about fasting. She told me to drink water to stay hydrated and if I got to the point where I felt sick, to drink a smoothie or something with nutrients. I decided to fast the very next day while spending some time studying the scripture she gave me. All day I read through Mark 9 about the story of the man possessed by a demon and God casted the demon out. I could not figure out what Mark 9:29 had to do with me. I had my fair share of things to work through, but I was not dealing with anything near what the person in the story was dealing with. I may have just been *hangry*, but I was frustrated with not being able to make the connection. It wasn't until my prayer time right before breaking the fast that I got the revelation: "Some things only come through prayer and fasting." It's not about the details of the 'Mark 9' story, it's that nothing happened for the possessed man until they fasted and prayed. That was the lesson God wanted me to learn and it has become a part of my strategy ever since.

I want it to become a part of yours too. After fasting that day, I got so much clarity and direction from God that I had been wanting and anticipating. I needed to fast and pray in order to receive it. God is such the perfect parent. If he would've given me everything I asked for in my prayers, I wouldn't have understood the importance of fasting. Not too long after that, God told me I needed to fast weekly for a year.

Ever since then, I fast every single week. I chose Monday as my day of choice because I want to start my week close to God. With that in mind, now Mondays have become my favorite day of the week. It's like that special alone time you get with your parent while all of your siblings are away. It's on my fasting days that God gives me the biggest instructions for my business and next steps I need to take for other areas of my life. On Mondays I get to silence my anxiousness to get to work and humble myself before God and get into alignment with what He needs from me.

Over the course of time, I have done tons of research on the logistics of fasting: When can I drink? What can I drink? What are the best times to fast? What are the different types of fasting? Once, it seemed like I had a million tabs open in research to find out how to somehow crack the 'cheat code' to fasting. God didn't need me to do any of that, he simply needed me to deny my flesh and feed my spirit so I would draw closer to him. A lot of you may be like me, searching for all of the answers to get things right on your walk with God. God just wants you. He wants your heart, He wants you to draw close to Him, and seek Him in all you do. That's it. In the words of Lauryn Hill, "It could all be so simple. But we rather make it hard."

As you grow and learn how to make God the CEO of your life, add fasting to the equation. Create a habit out of denying your flesh and feeding your spirit. If there has been something you have been praying for and you find that you are not receiving answers, remember what God

told me: Some things only come through prayer and
fasting.

Chapter 8: Now What?

CHAPTER 8:

Now What?

Have you ever felt like you've been pumped up to do nothing? I find that many who set out to inspire and motivate leave a huge cliff hanger as it relates to the 'Now what' factor. I don't want you to have read this entire book, gotten to the point where you understand the power of God as it relates to both your life and your business, but don't know how to apply it. Here is practically how you can make God the CEO of your business and more importantly, keep Him there. I am a fan of systems, so here is the formula to executing everything I have discussed in previous chapters.

Self-Awareness + Tunnel Vision + Goals +Action + Accountability

Self-Awareness

Excellence is one of my personal core values. One of my strengths that I truly thank God for is the ability to be self-aware. I am so passionate about being my best self. I am always looking for ways to improve. When I was younger, it would present itself in not-so positive ways. Instead of pursuing excellence, I strived for perfection which often left me disappointed and constantly letting myself down. As I got older I realized it's not about being perfect, but rather it is about being committed to growth and giving myself the freedom to sometimes make mistakes. So now, I use my commitment to excellence to consistently look for areas I can improve in, and work on them in my own time.

A few months ago, I realized that in the future, I was going to need a team in business. I have big business ideas, while also having a desire to be present with my husband and future children. I realized that in order for me to manage both of my personal and professional goals, I would need to, at some point, build a team. Not just any team, but a team that functions in excellence and drives results, even when I am not around. I realized that I didn't know how to build that type of team. I could've read a book, but I was more interested in hearing real stories instead of theories.

One of my favorite motivational speakers to listen to is Eric Thomas. Through his podcast, I have been able to get to know members of his team and get an inside listen at the mindset that made E.T. one of the number one motivational speakers in the world, and build the company to be a multi-million dollar brand. When he tells his story, he always talks about his right hand men, Karl and C.J., and how together they took his brand and company from nothing to thriving. When they announced they were doing an event called Take Control for entrepreneurs, I knew that I had to attend. I needed to learn how this team was able to function and grow to the level they have.

One of the stand-out presentations that day was by a man name Chris Daniel. Chris is a consultant and corporate trainer specializing in Project Management Professional (PMP) training who used a dynamic assessment called the Four Animal Assessment. His presentation was about self-awareness being the key to success and he demonstrated it through this animal assessment. The animal assessment uses the popular DISC personality assessment to describe various aspects of a person's personality and how to build a team that is effective. What I loved about it the most was how it didn't tell you to change your weaknesses, rather it told you how to use others in your team to build around them to minimize leaks in an organization. The assessment can be used not only for business, but for personal relationships as well. After the conference, I bought the assessment immediately to get a better understanding of how I need to build a team in the future.

Aside from professionally, self-awareness has allowed me to thrive as a woman and in my relationship with God. When I first wanted to grow spiritually, I had to come to terms with my trust issues about trusting a God I couldn't see because I couldn't trust the people who I could see. Or I couldn't trust the people who said they were representatives of God. By identifying the problem,

I was able to pray against it and ask God to show me who He is. And through his word, and spending time with Him, I realized God is the most deserving of my trust and people will always be flawed. Just as I am and just as He loves me in my flaws, I have to love others as well.

In today's world of social media, we are bombarded with pretty pictures and what seems to be others' perfect lives. Moms seem to have perfected a career, family life, and do it all while maintaining the perfect figure and making delicious vegan meals three times a day. That subconsciously tells the mom who is rightfully overwhelmed that something is wrong with her for being tired. The stress of not measuring up to the unrealistic picture being painted makes the situation worse. Now, instead of using self-awareness to figure out how to put controls in place to make life more manageable, you beat yourself up. Self-awareness allows you to admit to who you truly are while giving you the freedom to improve the areas you aren't happy with. Self-awareness alleviates the stress or pressure to be perfect.

Homework: Write down 4 weaknesses you have identified about yourself (2 personal and 2 business)

1.

2.

3.

4

Tunnel Vision

One day I turned on the television and a horse race was on. I was in my phone, so I wasn't fully attentive initially. Eventually, I decided to look up. I was curious as to why the horses had black, leather patches on the sides of their head next to their eyes. I thought, Why would they want to obstruct the horses' visions if they needed it to win the race? Since I knew nothing about being an equestrian, I did what any other curious millennial would do – I googled it.

In my search, I found that the leather patches were actually called blinders. Blinders are put on horses so they can focus on what is in front of them, and not get distracted by other forces such as the crowd or the other horses next to them during the race.

Horses are animals that are prey, instead of being hunters. For this reason, they naturally have peripheral vision so they can better protect themselves. Even while looking straight ahead, a horse can see what is on the side of them. Humans also have peripheral vision. The visual field of the human eye spans approximately 120 degrees of arc. Most of this is peripheral vision. If you want to test it out, try right now. As you're looking on the pages of this book, can you still see what's to the left of you? If someone was to the left of you waving right now, would you see it? The answer is most likely yes. Unfortunately, we don't have the luxury of putting on blinders to eliminate distractions. We have to work a little bit harder to stay focused on our own race.

Before we figure out how to stay focused, we must first identify and qualify what we are focusing on.

Identifying the focal point

Tunnel vision is defined as defective sight in which objects cannot be properly seen if not close to the center of the field of view. Synonyms for it include narrow focus, concentration, and fixation. I am a naturally ambitious person. For most of my life, I would say I had tunnel vision. I always focused on getting ahead or accomplishing a goal I had set for myself. When I was in high school, I was fixated on getting out of my parents' house. When I got to college, I was fixated on doing everything I could to graduate on time, with good grades, and secure a job in my field after graduation. When I started in the corporate world, I realized I was destined for more, then became fixated on getting my freedom back. When I started my first business, I became fixated on being self-employed. When I became self-employed, I was then fixated on making my first six-figures. You get it now, right?

My tunnel vision may have changed, but I was always laser focused on something. It wasn't until I began to grow in my relationship with God that I realized I got it all wrong. Tunnel vision isn't about being fixated on my goals. It may have worked out in the temporary to eliminate the distraction of friends, family, social media, etc., to reach my goals. All of these things, and more, that I zoned in on were all able to be accomplished. I eventually realized I was still getting it wrong. I didn't need to be fixated on my next goal or accomplishment. I needed to be fixated on God.

Proverbs 3:5 (*KJV*) says, "Trust in the Lord with your whole heart and lean not on your own understanding." The reason why I had been wrong in my tunnel vision all of those years is because I was focused on what I wanted and not what God wanted for me. Imagine if when you pass away and go to heaven, God greets you and reviews your life. You accomplished so many great things, had all these awards, money, and successful businesses. Then God shows you what He had planned for your life and everything you were so proud of was only an ounce of what He had for you. I don't know about you, but that thought alone is enough for me to realize I don't want that to happen to me. I read a statistic recently that says 98% of people die without realizing their dreams. There are also studies that show the 2% who do and become super successful are prone to depression and other mental illnesses. This is proof that success does not equal money. Of course it's always easier to say that after you're already successful. It's a little harder to believe money and success isn't everything when you don't have either. Tunnel vision is being focused on God, just as we went over in Chapter 5. Now that you have your new focal point, it's time to put blinders on, just as the horses did.

Homework: List what is currently distracting you from focusing on God

Goal Setting

Taking into consideration everything you have written down thus far, your goals are your intended results. For example, if you wrote social media as one of your distractions, your goal can be to limit social media use to only one hour a day. Make sure your goals are S.M.A.R.T: specific, measurable, attainable, relevant, and timely.

It is important that you write these goals down. Studies show when goals are written down, they have a significantly higher chance of being achieved than those that aren't. Also, put these goals somewhere that you can see every day so you don't forget. We constantly have things bombarding us for our attention every day. Don't let your goals get caught up in the noise.

Homework: Write down all of your goals based on the previous exercises

Plan of Action

What are goals if we don't execute them? I'm sure like many of us, you start the new year off with a ton of new goals and declarations. About midway through the year, some, if not all the goals, have been pushed back to next year. It's taken me about three years to start working on the summer body I promised myself a long time ago. So, I get it. But when it comes to growing in God, we have no time to waste. Our lives are on the line. I don't want this to be a book that you just put down or pass along and never revisit what you've learned. It's time to make a plan to get it done!

Homework: Create a plan of action for your goals on a separate sheet of paper using the example below:

Goal: Spend time with God daily

Deadline: Ongoing

Activity to reach the goal: Wake up 30 minutes earlier to pray

Frequency: Every Morning at 6:00am

Resources Needed: Bible, Journal

Accountability

Let's face it, if we could do it on our own we would have already. Whenever you are creating new habits and pursuing your goals, it is important to have someone who understands and is on the journey with you to hold you accountable. For a while, I struggled with having accountability partners because I didn't want to be vulnerable with anyone, especially other women. I asked God to send me good, like-minded people who understood me to support me on my journey.

He sent me two of my good friends, Tiona and Tish, who have been instrumental in my growth. We have prayed together, celebrated together, fasted together and spent days strategizing about business. Anything I have told them I wanted to do, they have held me accountable. They provide a safe space for me to be a work in progress and I do the same for them. As entrepreneurs, it is often hard to find people who just 'get it'. It is even harder to find people who sincerely want to see you win with no strings attached. This is why it is important that you pray for God to send you those people. We also have to protect ourselves from people the devil will send in the form of mentors, coaches, friends, etc., and pray to God for discernment.

Homework: Pray for an accountability partner or utilize your current contacts to find one. Be sure to make sure they're God- approved.

Acknowledgements:

The completion of this book could not have been possible without the holy trinity: the father, the son, and the holy spirit. To my Lord and Savior Jesus Christ, thank you for being the perfect person. Thank you for dying on the cross for my sins. Thank you for showing me that it is okay to be misunderstood because so were you. To my God, who sent His only son on earth to die for our sins, I thank you for creating heaven, earth, and everything in between. Thank you for always being with me, even when I chose not to be with you. Thank you for always being the perfect father and friend, even when I turned my back on you. Thank you for filling me with the Holy Spirit, who guides me in all that I do.

To my soon-to-be-husband, BJ, I would like to thank you once again for your love, support, and commitment to aiding me in being all that God has called me to be. I would like to thank my parents, Tim and Lolita Harrison. Without you there is no me. I am a perfect blend of the best sides of the both of you and I hope to make you proud. To my grandmother, whose prayers are the reason I have become who I am today. Thank you for always loving me and reminding me to seek God in all things. To my favorite auntie, Nese, thank you for always understanding me and being there for me when I need you. Your love, advice, guidance, and support have carried me through many of my darkest moments. I know for sure that I can always count on you. My sister, Jalysa, we are sisters by blood and best friends by choice. Thank you for always cheering me on. To my girl Tiona, thank you for allowing God to use you. You have taught me so much about being a woman of God just by being you. You have planted seeds that God has watered. I am so blessed to have you in my life. Tish, thank you for being the best life coach friend I could ask for. You have always helped me keep things in perspective and make sure in the midst of all of this ambition, I take time out for myself too. To my business coach, Raevyn, thank you for being an example that God and business don't have to be separate. Your obedience to your calling, made me a lot more comfortable in being obedient to mine. Last but MOST DEFINITELY not least. To the Blessed + Bossed Up Tribe all over the world who listen to my podcast THANK YOU. Being called is not easy, but the way you all support me and uplift me without ever even meeting me is the most amazing feeling in the world.

Made in the USA
Columbia, SC
19 September 2018